Born in 2015

by

Kerry Butters.

Born in 2015

Millennium:	3rd millennium
Centuries:	20th century – **21st century** – 22nd century
Decades:	1980s 1990s 2000s – **2010s** – 2020s 2030s 2040s
Years:	2012 2013 2014 – **2015** – 2016 2017 2018

2015 (MMXV) was a common year starting on Thursday (dominical letter D) of the Gregorian calendar, the 2015th year of the Common Era (CE) and *Anno Domini* (AD) designations, the 15th year of the 3rd millennium, the 15th year of the 21st century, and the 6th year of the **2010s** decade.

2015 was designated as:

- International Year of Light
- International Year of Soils

4

Contents

Events

January

- January 1
  - The Eurasian Economic Union comes into effect, creating a political and economic union between Russia, Belarus, Armenia, Kazakhstan and Kyrgyzstan.
  - Lithuania officially adopts the euro as its currency, replacing the litas, and becomes the nineteenth Eurozone country.
- January 3–7 – A series of massacres in Baga, Nigeria and surrounding villages by Boko Haram kills more than 2,000 people.
- January 15 – The Swiss National Bank abandons the cap on the franc's value relative to the euro, causing turmoil in international financial markets.

- January 22 – After Houthi forces seize the presidential palace, Yemeni President Abd Rabbuh Mansur Hadi resigns after months of unrest.

February

- February 12
  - Leaders from Russia, Ukraine, Germany and France reach an agreement on the conflict in eastern Ukraine that includes a ceasefire and withdrawal of heavy weapons. However, several days later, the Ukrainian government and pro-Russian rebels claim that, within its first day, the ceasefire was broken 139 times, as both sides failed to withdraw their heavy weapons and fighting had continued.
  - The United Nations Security Council adopts Resolution 2199 to combat terrorism.
- February 16 – The Egyptian military begins conducting airstrikes against a branch of the Islamic militant group ISIL in Libya in retaliation for the group's beheading of over a dozen Egyptian Christians.

March

- March 5–8 – The ancient city sites of Nimrud, Hatra and Dur-Sharrukin in Iraq are demolished by the Islamic State of Iraq and the Levant.
- March 6 – NASA's *Dawn* probe enters orbit around Ceres, becoming the first spacecraft to visit a dwarf planet.
- March 12 – The Islamic State of Iraq and the Levant becomes allies with fellow jihadist group Boko Haram, effectively annexing the group.
- March 24 – An Airbus A320-211 operated by Germanwings crashes in the French Alps, killing all 150 on board.
- March 25 – A Saudi Arabia-led coalition of Arab countries starts a military intervention in Yemen in order to uphold the Yemeni government in its fight against the Houthis' southern offensive.

April

- April 2 – 148 people are killed, the majority students, in a mass shooting at the Garissa University College in Kenya, perpetrated by the militant terrorist organization Al-Shabaab.
- April 25 – A magnitude 7.8 earthquake strikes Nepal and causes 8,857 deaths in Nepal, 130 in India, 27 in

China and 4 in Bangladesh with a total of 9,018 deaths.
- April 29 – The World Health Organization (WHO) declares that rubella has been eradicated from the Americas.

May

- May 1–October 31 – Expo 2015 is held in Milan, Italy.
- May 11–12 – *Version O* of *Les Femmes d'Alger* by Pablo Picasso sells for US$179.3 million at Christie's auction in New York, while the sculpture *L'Homme au doigt* by Alberto Giacometti sells for US$141.3 million, setting a new world record for a painting and for a sculpture, respectively.
- May 12 – A second major earthquake in Nepal, measuring 7.3 on the moment magnitude scale, results in 153 deaths in Nepal, 62 in India, 1 in China and 2 in Bangladesh with a total of 218 deaths.
- May 23 – Ireland votes to legalize same-sex marriage, becoming the first country to legalize same-sex marriage by popular vote.

June

- June 2 – FIFA President Sepp Blatter announces his intention to resign amidst an FBI-led corruption investigation, and calls for an extraordinary congress to elect a new president as soon as possible.

- June 6 – The governments of India and Bangladesh officially ratify their 1974 agreement to exchange enclaves along their border.
- June 7–8 – The 41st G7 summit is held in Schloss Elmau, Bavaria.
- June 25–26 – ISIL claim responsibility for three attacks around the world during the Ramadan:
  - Kobanî massacre: ISIL fighters detonate three car bombs, enter Kobanî, Syria, and open fire at civilians, killing more than 220.
  - Sousse attacks: 22-year-old Seifeddine Rezgui opens fire at a tourist resort at Port El Kantaoui, Tunisia, killing 40 people.
  - Kuwait mosque bombing: A suicide bomber attacks the Shia Mosque Imam Ja'far as-Sadiq at Kuwait City, Kuwait, killing 27 people and injuring 227 others.
- June 30
  - Cuba becomes the first country in the world to eradicate mother-to-child transmission of HIV and syphilis.
  - A Lockheed C-130 Hercules operated by the Indonesian Air Force crashed into a crowded residential neighborhood in Medan shortly after

take-off from Soewondo Air Force Base, killing 143 people including 22 others on the ground, marking the second-deadliest air disaster to ever occur in Medan and the deadliest crash in Indonesian Air Force peacetime history.

July

- July 1 – Greek government-debt crisis: Greece becomes the first advanced economy to miss a payment to the International Monetary Fund in the 71-year history of the IMF.
- July 14
  - NASA's *New Horizons* spacecraft performs a close flyby of Pluto, becoming the first spacecraft in history to visit the distant world.
  - Iran agrees to long-term limits of its nuclear program in exchange for sanctions relief.
- July 20 – Cuba and the United States reestablish full diplomatic relations, ending a 54-year stretch of hostility between the nations.
- July 24 – Turkey begins a series of airstrikes against PKK and ISIL targets after the 2015 Suruç bombing.

August

- August 5 – Debris found on Réunion Island is confirmed to be that of Malaysian Airlines Flight 370, missing since March 2014.
- August 17 – A bombing takes place inside the Erawan Shrine at the Ratchaprasong intersection in Pathum Wan District, Bangkok, Thailand, killing 20 people and injuring 125.

September

- September 10 – Scientists announce the discovery of *Homo naledi*, a previously unknown species of early human in South Africa.
- September 14 – Gravitational waves are detected for the first time, by LIGO. This is not announced until February 11 2016.
- September 18 – Automaker Volkswagen is alleged to have been involved in worldwide rigging of diesel emissions tests, affecting an estimated 11 million vehicles globally.
- September 24 – A stampede during the Hajj pilgrimage in Mecca, Saudi Arabia, kills at least 2,200 people and injures more than 900 others, with more than 650 missing.

- September 28 – NASA announces that liquid water has been found on Mars.
- September 30 – Russia begins air strikes against ISIL and anti-government forces in Syria in support of the Syrian government.

October

- October 3 – A United States airstrike on a Médecins Sans Frontières (Doctors Without Borders) hospital in Afghanistan accidentally kills an estimated 20 people.
- October 10 – A suicide bomb kills at least 100 people at a peace rally in Ankara, Turkey, and injures more than 400 others.
- October 23 – Hurricane Patricia becomes the most intense hurricane ever recorded in the Western Hemisphere, with winds of 200 mph and a pressure of 879 mbar.
- October 26 – A magnitude 7.5 earthquake strikes the Hindu Kush region and causes 398 deaths, with 279 in Pakistan, 115 in Afghanistan and 4 in India.
- October 31 – Flight KGL9268, an Airbus A321 airliner en route to Saint Petersburg from Sharm el-Sheikh, crashes near Al-Hasana in Sinai, killing all 217 passengers and 7 crew members on board.

November

- November 7 – Chinese and Taiwanese presidents, Xi Jinping and Ma Ying-jeou, formally meet for the first time.
- November 12 – Several suicide bombings occur in Beirut, Lebanon, killing 43 and injuring 239. The Islamic State in Iraq and the Levant claim responsibility.
- November 13 – Multiple terrorist attacks claimed by Islamic State of Iraq and the Levant (ISIL) in Paris, France, resulting in 130 fatalities.
- November 24 – Syrian Civil War: Turkey shoots down a Russian fighter jet in the first case of a NATO member destroying a Russian aircraft since the 1950s.
- November 30 – The 2015 United Nations Climate Change Conference (COP 21) is held in Paris, attended by leaders from 147 nations.

December

- December 12 – A global climate change pact is agreed at the COP 21 summit, committing all countries to reduce carbon emissions for the first time.
- December 22 – SpaceX lands a Falcon 9 rocket, the first reusable rocket to successfully enter orbital space and return.

Births

- May 2 – Princess Charlotte of Cambridge
- June 15 – Prince Nicolas, Duke of Ångermanland

Deaths

January

Mario Cuomo

King Abdullah of Saudi Arabia

Zhelyu Zhelev

Richard von Weizsäcker

- January 1
  - Ulrich Beck, German sociologist (b. 1944)
  - Mario Cuomo, American politician (b. 1932)
  - Omar Karami, 58th Prime Minister of Lebanon (b. 1934)
  - Boris Morukov, Russian astronaut (b. 1950)
- January 3 – Edward Brooke, American politician (b. 1919)
- January 4 – Pino Daniele, Italian singer, songwriter, and guitarist (b. 1955)
- January 5 – Jean-Pierre Beltoise, French race car driver (b. 1937)
- January 6 – Vlastimil Bubník, Czech ice hockey player and footballer (b. 1931)
- January 7
  - Tadeusz Konwicki, Polish writer and film director (b. 1926)
  - Rod Taylor, Australian actor (b. 1930)

- January 8 – Andraé Crouch, American singer, songwriter, and pastor (b. 1942)
- January 9 – Józef Oleksy, 7th Prime Minister of Poland (b. 1946)
- January 10 – Francesco Rosi, Italian film director (b. 1922)
- January 11
  - Jenő Buzánszky, Hungarian footballer (b. 1925)
  - Anita Ekberg, Swedish actress (b. 1931)
- January 12 – Elena Obraztsova, Russian opera singer (b. 1939)
- January 17 – Faten Hamama, Egyptian actress (b. 1931)
- January 20
  - Edgar Froese, German musician (b. 1944)
  - Hitoshi Saito, Japanese judoka (b. 1961)
- January 21 – Leon Brittan, British politician (b. 1939)
- January 23 – King Abdullah of Saudi Arabia (b. 1924)
- January 24 – Otto Carius, German WWII tank commander (b. 1922)
- January 25 – Demis Roussos, Greek singer (b. 1946)
- January 27 – Charles Hard Townes, American Nobel physicist (b. 1915)
- January 28 – Yves Chauvin, French Nobel chemist (b. 1930)

- January 29 – Colleen McCullough, Australian writer (b. 1937)
- January 30
  - Carl Djerassi, American chemist (b. 1923)
  - Geraldine McEwan, British actress (b. 1932)
  - Zhelyu Zhelev, 1st President of Bulgaria (b. 1935)
- January 31
  - Lizabeth Scott, American actress (b. 1922)
  - Richard von Weizsäcker, President of Germany (b. 1920)

February

Aldo Ciccolini

André Brink

Clark Terry

Leonard Nimoy

- February 1
  - Aldo Ciccolini, Italian-born French pianist (b. 1925)

- Udo Lattek, German footballer and coach (b. 1935)
- February 3 – Martin Gilbert, English historian (b. 1936)
- February 5
  - Henri Coppens, Belgian footballer and coach (b. 1930)
  - Val Logsdon Fitch, American Nobel physicist (b. 1923)
- February 6
  - André Brink, South African writer (b. 1935)
  - Assia Djebar, Algerian writer (b. 1936)
- February 7 – Marshall Rosenberg, American psychologist and writer (b. 1934)
- February 10 – Karl Josef Becker, German cardinal (b. 1928)
- February 12 – Movita Castaneda, American actress (b. 1916)
- February 14
  - Michele Ferrero, Italian businessman (b. 1925)
  - Louis Jourdan, French actor (b. 1921)
  - Franjo Mihalić, Croatian-Serbian athlete and coach (b. 1920)
  - Wim Ruska, Dutch wrestler and martial artist (b. 1940)
- February 16

- ○ Lesley Gore, American singer (b. 1946)
  - ○ Lorena Rojas, Mexican actress (b. 1971)
- February 18 – Claude Criquielion, Belgian road bicycle racer (b. 1957)
- February 21
  - ○ Aleksei Gubarev, Russian cosmonaut (b. 1931)
  - ○ Clark Terry, American jazz trumpeter and fugelhornist (b. 1920)
- February 27
  - ○ Boris Nemtsov, Russian politician (b. 1959)
  - ○ Leonard Nimoy, American actor (b. 1931)
- February 28
  - ○ Yaşar Kemal, Turkish author (b. 1923)
  - ○ Anthony Mason, American basketball player (b. 1966)

March

Sam Simon

Terry Pratchett

Malcolm Fraser

Lee Kuan Yew

- March 1
  - Joshua Fishman, American linguist (b. 1926)
  - Wolfram Wuttke, German footballer (b. 1961)
- March 2 – Dave Mackay, Scottish footballer and coach (b. 1934)
- March 5 – Edward Egan, American cardinal (b. 1932)
- March 7 – Yoshihiro Tatsumi, Japanese manga artist (b. 1935)
- March 8 – Sam Simon, American producer and philanthropist (b. 1955)
- March 9
  - Camille Muffat, French swimmer (b. 1989)
  - Frei Otto, German architect (b. 1925)
  - Alexis Vastine, French boxer (b. 1986)
- March 11 – Walter Burkert, German academic and writer (b. 1931)
- March 12
  - Michael Graves, American architect (b. 1934)
  - Terry Pratchett, English writer (b. 1948)
- March 13 – Daevid Allen, Australian musician (b. 1938)
- March 14 – Valentin Rasputin, Russian writer (b. 1937)
- March 15
  - Xu Caihou, Chinese army general (b. 1943)
  - Mike Porcaro, American bass guitarist (b. 1955)

- March 16 – Andy Fraser, English songwriter and bass guitarist (b. 1952)
- March 19 – Gerda van der Kade-Koudijs, Dutch athlete (b. 1923)
- March 20 – Malcolm Fraser, 22nd Prime Minister of Australia (b. 1930)
- March 21
  - Hans Erni, Swiss artist (b. 1909)
  - Jørgen Ingmann, Danish musician (b. 1925)
  - Alberta Watson, Canadian actress (b. 1955)
- March 23 – Lee Kuan Yew, 1st Prime Minister of Singapore (b. 1923)
- March 26
  - Dinkha IV, Iraqi patriarch (b. 1935)
  - Tomas Tranströmer, Swedish Nobel poet and translator (b. 1931)
- March 27 – Olga Syahputra, Indonesian actor and singer (b. 1983)
- March 29 – Miroslav Ondříček, Czech cinematographer (b. 1934)
- March 30 – Ingrid van Houten-Groeneveld, Dutch astronomer (b. 1921)

April

Günter Grass

Percy Sledge

Verne Gagne

- April 2 – Manoel de Oliveira, Portuguese film director and screenwriter (b. 1908)
- April 4 – Klaus Rifbjerg, Danish author (b. 1931)
- April 6 – James Best, American actor (b. 1926)
- April 7 – Geoffrey Lewis, American actor (b. 1935)
- April 8 – Jean-Claude Turcotte, Canadian cardinal (b. 1936)
- April 10 – Rose Francine Rogombé, Gabonese lawyer and politician (b. 1942)

- April 13
  - Eduardo Galeano, Uruguayan writer (b. 1940)
  - Günter Grass, German Nobel writer (b. 1927)
  - Thelma Coyne Long, Australian tennis player (b. 1918)
- April 14
  - Percy Sledge, American singer (b. 1940)
  - Roberto Tucci, Italian cardinal (b. 1921)
- April 15 – Surya Bahadur Thapa, 24th Prime Minister of Nepal (b. 1928)
- April 16 – Stanislav Gross, 5th Prime Minister of the Czech Republic (b. 1969)
- April 17 – Francis George, American cardinal (b. 1937)
- April 24 – Władysław Bartoszewski, Polish politician and resistance fighter (b. 1922)

- April 27
  - Verne Gagne, American professional wrestler (b. 1926)
  - Andrew Lesnie, Australian cinematographer (b. 1956)
- April 29 – Giovanni Canestri, Italian cardinal (b. 1918)
- April 30
  - Ben E. King, American singer (b. 1938)
  - Patachou, French singer and actress (b. 1918)

May

Maya Plisetskaya

B.B. King

John Forbes Nash, Jr.

- May 1
  - Geoff Duke, British motorcycle racer (b. 1923)
  - Grace Lee Whitney, American actress and singer (b. 1930)
- May 2
  - Maya Plisetskaya, Russian ballet dancer, choreographer, ballet director, and actress (b. 1925)

- o Ruth Rendell, British author (b. 1930)
- May 9 – Kenan Evren, Turkish military officer, seventh President of Turkey (b. 1917)
- May 10 – Chris Burden, American artist (b. 1946)
- May 12 – Peter Gay, American psychohistorian (b. 1923)
- May 14 – B.B. King, American singer-songwriter and guitarist (b. 1925)
- May 15 – Renzo Zorzi, Italian racing driver (b. 1946)
- May 18
  - o Halldór Ásgrímsson, Prime Minister of Iceland (b. 1947)
  - o Raymond Gosling, British scientist (b. 1926)
- May 19 – Gerald Götting, German politician (b. 1923)
- May 21 – Annarita Sidoti, Italian race walker (b. 1969)
- May 23
  - o Anne Meara, American actress and comedian (b. 1929)
  - o John Forbes Nash, Jr., American Nobel mathematician (b. 1928)
- May 24 – Tanith Lee, British writer (b. 1947)
- May 25 – Mary Ellen Mark, American photographer (b. 1940)
- May 26 – Vicente Aranda, Spanish film director (b. 1926)

- May 27 – Nils Christie, Norwegian criminologist (b. 1928)
- May 29
  - Henry Carr, American sprinter (b. 1941)
  - Doris Hart, American tennis player (b. 1925)
  - Betsy Palmer, American actress (b. 1926)

June

Nicholas Liverpool

Christopher Lee

Yevgeny Primakov

Chris Squire

- June 1
    - Charles Kennedy, British politician (b. 1959)
    - Nicholas Liverpool, Dominican politician, sixth President of Dominica (b. 1934)
- June 2 – Irwin Rose, American Nobel biochemist (b. 1926)
- June 4 – Hermann Zapf, German typeface designer (b. 1918)
- June 5 – Tariq Aziz, Iraqi politician (b. 1936)
- June 6 – Pierre Brice, French actor (b. 1929)
- June 7 – Christopher Lee, English actor (b. 1922)
- June 9 – James Last, German composer and big band leader (b. 1929)
- June 11
    - Ornette Coleman, American free jazz saxophonist (b. 1930)
    - Ron Moody, British actor (b. 1924)
    - Dusty Rhodes, American professional wrestler (b. 1945)
    -

- June 14
  - Qiao Shi, Chinese politician (b. 1924)
  - Zito, Brazilian footballer (b. 1932)
- June 15
  - Jeanna Friske, Russian singer, model, and actress (b. 1974)
  - Kirk Kerkorian, American businessman (b. 1917)
- June 16 – Charles Correa, Indian architect (b. 1930)
- June 17
  - Ron Clarke, Australian runner (b. 1937)
  - Süleyman Demirel, Turkish politician, ninth President of Turkey (b. 1924)
  - Roberto M. Levingston, Argentine general and politician, 36th President of Argentina (b. 1920)
- June 20 – Esther Brand, South African athlete (b. 1922)
- June 21
  - Veijo Meri, Finnish writer (b. 1928)
  - Gunther Schuller, American composer, conductor, historian, and jazz musician (b. 1925)
- June 22
  - Laura Antonelli, Italian actress (b. 1941)
  - James Horner, American film composer (b. 1953)
- June 23
  - Magali Noël, French actress and singer (b. 1931)
  - Dick Van Patten, American actor (b. 1928)
- June 25

- ○ Nerses Bedros XIX Tarmouni, Armenian Catholic Patriarch of Cilicia (b. 1940)
  - ○ Patrick Macnee, English actor (b. 1922)
- June 26 – Yevgeny Primakov, Russian politician and diplomat, Prime Minister of Russia from 1998 to 1999 (b. 1929)
- June 27 – Chris Squire, English bass guitarist (b. 1948)
- June 29
  - ○ Josef Masopust, Czech football player and coach (b. 1931)
  - ○ Charles Pasqua, French politician (b. 1927)

July

Omar Sharif

Satoru Iwata

A. P. J. Abdul Kalam

- July 1
    - Sergio Sollima, Italian film director (b. 1921)
    - Nicholas Winton, British humanitarian (b. 1909)
- July 5 – Yoichiro Nambu, Japanese-American Nobel physicist (b. 1921)
- July 10
    - Roger Rees, Welsh-American actor (b. 1944)
    - Omar Sharif, Egyptian actor (b. 1932)
    - Jon Vickers, Canadian tenor (b. 1926)
- July 11
    - Giacomo Biffi, Italian cardinal (b. 1928)
    - Patricia Crone, Danish scholar (b. 1945)
    - Satoru Iwata, Japanese businessman and video game programmer (b. 1959)
- July 12 – Chenjerai Hove, Zimbabwean poet (b. 1956)
- July 13 – Martin Litchfield West, British classical scholar (b. 1937)
- July 14 – Ildikó Schwarczenberger, Hungarian fencer (b. 1951)
- July 15 – Wan Li, Chinese politician (b. 1916)

- July 16 – Alcides Ghiggia, Uruguayan footballer (b. 1926)
- July 17 – Jules Bianchi, French race car driver (b. 1989)
- July 18 – Alex Rocco, American actor (b. 1936)
- July 19 – Galina Prozumenshchikova, Soviet swimmer (b. 1948)
- July 21
    - Theodore Bikel, Austrian-American actor (b. 1924)
    - E. L. Doctorow, American author (b. 1931)
- July 23 – William Wakefield Baum, American Catholic cardinal (b. 1926)
- July 27 – A. P. J. Abdul Kalam, Indian scientist and politician, 11th President of India (b. 1931)
- July 28 – Edward Natapei, 6th Prime Minister of Vanuatu (b. 1954)
- July 30
    - Lynn Anderson, American country singer (b. 1947)
    - Alena Vrzáňová, Czech figure skater (b. 1931)
- July 31 – Roddy Piper, Canadian wrestler (b. 1954)

August

Robert Conquest

Yvonne Craig

Oliver Sacks

- August 1 – Cilla Black, English singer and entertainer (b. 1943)
- August 3 – Robert Conquest, British-born American historian (b. 1917)
- August 7
  - Manuel Contreras, Chilean general (b. 1929)
  - Frances Oldham Kelsey, Canadian physician (b. 1914)

- August 9 – John Henry Holland, American computer scientist (b. 1929)
- August 11 – Harald Nielsen, Danish footballer (b. 1941)
- August 12 – Jaakko Hintikka, Finnish philosopher and logician (b. 1929)
- August 14 – Bob Johnston, American record producer (b. 1932)
- August 16 – Mile Mrkšić, Serbian military officer (b. 1947)
- August 17
  - Jacob Bekenstein, Mexican theoretical physicist (b. 1947)
  - Yvonne Craig, American actress (b. 1937)
  - Arsen Dedić, Croatian musician (b. 1938)
  - László Paskai, Hungarian cardinal (b. 1927)
- August 20 – Egon Bahr, German politician (b. 1922)
- August 22
  - Ieng Thirith, Cambodian politician (b. 1932)
  - Eric Thompson, English racing driver (b. 1919)
- August 23 – Guy Ligier, French racing driver and team owner (b. 1930)
- August 24 – Justin Wilson, British racing driver (b. 1978)
- August 29 – Wayne Dyer, American author and motivational speaker (b. 1940)

- August 30
  - Wes Craven, American film director and writer (b. 1939)
  - Oliver Sacks, British-American neurologist and writer (b. 1933)

September

Jackie Collins

Yogi Berra

- September 1 – Dean Jones, American actor (b. 1931)
- September 3 – Chandra Bahadur Dangi, Nepalese dwarf, world's shortest man (b. 1939)
- September 4 – Rico Rodriguez, Cuban-British musician (b. 1934)

- September 5 – Setsuko Hara, Japanese actress (b. 1920)
- September 7 – Candida Royalle, American actress and director (b. 1950)
- September 10 – Adrian Frutiger, Swiss typeface designer (b. 1928)
- September 12 – Ron Springett, British footballer (b. 1935)
- September 13 – Moses Malone, American basketball player (b. 1955)
- September 14 – Corneliu Vadim Tudor, Romanian politician (b. 1949)
- September 17 – Dettmar Cramer, German football coach (b. 1925)
- September 19 – Jackie Collins, British novelist (b. 1937)
- September 22 – Yogi Berra, American baseball player (b. 1925)
- September 23 – Dragan Holcer, Croatian footballer (b. 1945)
- September 27
  - John Guillermin, British film director and producer (b. 1925)
  - Pietro Ingrao, Italian politician (b. 1915)
- September 28 – Ignacio Zoco, Spanish footballer (b. 1939)

- September 29 – Phil Woods, American saxophonist (b. 1931)

October

Denis Healey

Henning Mankell

Richard F. Heck

Maureen O'Hara

- October 2
  - Eric Arturo Delvalle, Panamanian politician (b. 1937)
  - Brian Friel, Irish playwright (b. 1929)
- October 3 – Denis Healey, British politician (b. 1917)
- October 5
  - Chantal Akerman, Belgian filmmaker (b. 1950)
  - Infante Carlos, Spanish nobleman (b. 1938)
  - Henning Mankell, Swedish author (b. 1948)
- October 6 – Árpád Göncz, Hungarian politician, President of Hungary (b. 1922)
- October 7
  - Dominique Dropsy, French footballer (b. 1951)
  - Harry Gallatin, American basketball player and coach (b. 1927)
  - Jurelang Zedkaia, Fifth President of the Marshall Islands (b. 1950)
- October 9 – Geoffrey Howe, British politician (b. 1926)
- October 10 – Richard F. Heck, American chemist (b. 1931)
- October 12 – Joan Leslie, American actress (b. 1925)
- October 14
  - Nurlan Balgimbayev, Kazakh politician (b. 1947)
  - Mathieu Kérékou, Fifth President of Benin (b. 1933)
  -

- October 17
    - Danièle Delorme, French actress (b. 1926)
    - Howard Kendall, English footballer and manager (b. 1946)
- October 18 – Gamal El-Ghitani, Egyptian author (b. 1945)
- October 19 – Ali Treki, Libyan diplomat (b. 1938)
- October 23 – Paride Tumburus, Italian footballer (b. 1939)
- October 24
    - Ján Chryzostom Korec, Slovakian Jesuit Cardinal (b. 1924)
    - Maureen O'Hara, Irish-American actress (b. 1920)
- October 25 – Flip Saunders, American basketball player and coach (b. 1955)
- October 26 – Leo Kadanoff, American physicist (b. 1937)
- October 30 – Sinan Şamil Sam, Turkish boxer (b. 1974)
- October 31 – Ants Antson, Estonian speed skater (b. 1938)

November

Fred Thompson

Yitzhak Navon

Helmut Schmidt

Jonah Lomu

Kim Young-sam

- November 1
  - Günter Schabowski, German politician (b. 1929)
  - Fred Thompson, American politician and actor (b. 1942)
- November 3 – Ahmed Chalabi, Iraqi politician (b. 1944)
- November 4
  - René Girard, French-American historian (b. 1923)
  - Melissa Mathison, American screenwriter (b. 1950)
- November 5
  - Nora Brockstedt, Norwegian singer (b. 1923)
  - Czesław Kiszczak, Polish soldier and politician (b. 1925)
- November 7
  - Gunnar Hansen, Icelandic-American actor and author (b. 1947)
  - Yitzhak Navon, Israeli politician, President of Israel (b. 1921)
- November 8 – Andrei Eshpai, Russian pianist (b. 1925)

- November 9
  - Ernst Fuchs, Austrian painter (b. 1930)
  - Allen Toussaint, American musician (b. 1938)
  - Andy White, Scottish drummer (b. 1930)
- November 10
  - André Glucksmann, French philosopher (b. 1937)
  - Klaus Roth, British mathematician (b. 1925)
  - Helmut Schmidt, German politician, Chancellor of West Germany (b. 1918)
- November 11 – Phil Taylor, English rock drummer (b. 1954)
- November 12
  - Márton Fülöp, Hungarian footballer (b. 1983)
  - Jihadi John, Kuwaiti member of ISIS (b. 1988)
- November 15 – Saeed Jaffrey, Indian-British actor (b. 1929)
- November 18
  - Jonah Lomu, New Zealand rugby union player (b. 1975)
  - Mal Whitfield, American middle-distance runner (b. 1924)
- November 20 – Kitanoumi Toshimitsu, Japanese sumo wrestler (b. 1953)
- November 21
  - Bob Foster, American boxer (b. 1938)
  - Linda Haglund, Swedish sprinter (b. 1956)

- November 22 – Kim Young-sam, South Korean politician, President of South Korea (b. 1927)
- November 23 – Douglass North, American economist (b. 1920)
- November 28
  - Gerry Byrne, English footballer (b. 1938)
  - Barbro Hiort af Ornäs, Swedish actress (b. 1921)
- November 30
  - Fatema Mernissi, Moroccan feminist writer and sociologist (b. 1940)
  - Shigeru Mizuki, Japanese manga artist (b. 1922)
  - Eldar Ryazanov, Russian film director (b. 1927)

December

Robert Loggia

Kurt Masur

Haskell Wexler

Lemmy

- December 1 – Jim Loscutoff, American basketball player (b. 1930)
- December 2
  - Gabriele Ferzetti, Italian actor (b. 1925)
  - Ferenc Juhász, Hungarian poet (b. 1928)
- December 3 – Scott Weiland, American singer and musician (b. 1967)
- December 4
  - Erik De Vlaeminck, Belgian professional cyclist (b. 1945)
  - Robert Loggia, American actor (b. 1930)
  - Yossi Sarid, Israeli politician (b. 1940)

- December 5 – Dimitar Iliev Popov, Prime Minister of Bulgaria (1990-1991) (b. 1927)
- December 6 – Franzl Lang, German Yodeler (b. 1930)
- December 8 – Alan Hodgkinson, English footballer (b. 1936)
- December 9
  - Carlo Furno, Italian cardinal (b. 1921)
  - Julio Terrazas Sandoval, Bolivian cardinal (b. 1936)
- December 10
  - Arnold Peralta, Hondurian footballer (b. 1989)
  - Dolph Schayes, American basketball player and coach (b. 1928)
- December 13 – Benedict Anderson, American academic (b. 1936)
- December 15 – Licio Gelli, Italian financier (b. 1919)
- December 19
  - Jimmy Hill, English footballer and television presenter (b. 1928)
  - Kurt Masur, German conductor (b. 1927)
- December 23
  - Alfred G. Gilman, American pharmacologist and biochemist (b. 1941)
  - Don Howe, English footballer (b. 1935)
  - Bülent Ulusu, Prime Minister of Turkey (b. 1923)
  -

- December 27
  - Stein Eriksen, Norwegian alpine skier, Olympic champion (b. 1927)
  - Ellsworth Kelly, American artist (b. 1923)
  - Haskell Wexler, American cinematographer and film director (b. 1922)
- December 28
  - Eloy Inos, American politician, Governor of the Northern Mariana Islands (b. 1949)
  - Guru Josh, British musician (b. 1964)
  - Lemmy, British singer and bass guitarist (b. 1945)
  - Ian Murdock, German-American software programmer (b. 1973)
- December 29
  - Elżbieta Krzesińska, Polish athlete (b. 1934)
  - Pavel Srníček, Czech footballer (b. 1968)
- December 31
  - Natalie Cole, American singer (b. 1950)
  - Wayne Rogers, American actor (b. 1933)

Nobel Prizes

Nobel medal

- Chemistry – Paul L. Modrich; Aziz Sancar and Tomas Lindahl
- Economics – Angus Deaton
- Literature – Svetlana Alexievich
- Peace – Tunisian National Dialogue Quartet
- Physics – Takaaki Kajita and Arthur B. McDonald
- Physiology or Medicine – William C. Campbell, Satoshi Ōmura and Tu Youyou

In the News

2015 got off to a sad start with the Charlie Hebdo massacre in January, which saw gunmen kill 11 at the French satirical magazine.

In April the Hatton Garden heist gripped the nation, when a gang carried out what is thought to be the largest burglary in English legal history.

Alton Towers also hit the headlines in June, when the Smiler rollercoaster crashed seriously injuring five people.

July also saw American dentist Walter Palmer kill beloved lion Cecil in Zimbabwe - an act that caused outrage the world over.

2015 Calendar

2015 Calendar

January 2015						
M	Tu	W	Th	Fr	Sa	Su
			1	2	3	4
5	6	7	8	9	10	11
12	13	14	15	16	17	18
19	20	21	22	23	24	25
26	27	28	29	30	31	

February 2015						
M	Tu	W	Th	Fr	Sa	Su
						1
2	3	4	5	6	7	8
9	10	11	12	13	14	15
16	17	18	19	20	21	22
23	24	25	26	27	28	

March 2015						
M	Tu	W	Th	Fr	Sa	Su
						1
2	3	4	5	6	7	8
9	10	11	12	13	14	15
16	17	18	19	20	21	22
23	24	25	26	27	28	29
30	31					

April 2015						
M	Tu	W	Th	Fr	Sa	Su
		1	2	3	4	5
6	7	8	9	10	11	12
13	14	15	16	17	18	19
20	21	22	23	24	25	26
27	28	29	30			

August 2015						
M	Tu	W	Th	Fr	Sa	Su
					1	2
3	4	5	6	7	8	9
10	11	12	13	14	15	16
17	18	19	20	21	22	23
24	25	26	27	28	29	30
31						

December 2015						
M	Tu	W	Th	Fr	Sa	Su
	1	2	3	4	5	6
7	8	9	10	11	12	13
14	15	16	17	18	19	20
21	22	23	24	25	26	27
28	29	30	31			

May 2015						
M	Tu	W	Th	Fr	Sa	Su
				1	2	3
4	5	6	7	8	9	10
11	12	13	14	15	16	17
18	19	20	21	22	23	24
25	26	27	28	29	30	31

June 2015						
M	Tu	W	Th	Fr	Sa	Su
1	2	3	4	5	6	7
8	9	10	11	12	13	14
15	16	17	18	19	20	21
22	23	24	25	26	27	28
29	30					

July 2015						
M	Tu	W	Th	Fr	Sa	Su
		1	2	3	4	5
6	7	8	9	10	11	12
13	14	15	16	17	18	19
20	21	22	23	24	25	26
27	28	29	30	31		

September 2015						
M	Tu	W	Th	Fr	Sa	Su
	1	2	3	4	5	6
7	8	9	10	11	12	13
14	15	16	17	18	19	20
21	22	23	24	25	26	27
28	29	30				

October 2015						
M	Tu	W	Th	Fr	Sa	Su
			1	2	3	4
5	6	7	8	9	10	11
12	13	14	15	16	17	18
19	20	21	22	23	24	25
26	27	28	29	30	31	

November 2015						
M	Tu	W	Th	Fr	Sa	Su
						1
2	3	4	5	6	7	8
9	10	11	12	13	14	15
16	17	18	19	20	21	22
23	24	25	26	27	28	29
30